card tricks

card tricks

couplets

THOMAS TIMMINS

card tricks © 2020 Thomas Timmins
All rights reserved.

ISBN 978-0-9975112-9-1

Published by Zoëtown® Media
Zoëtown is registered trademark of Zoëtown Media.
Greenfield, MA
www.thomastimmins.com

Book and cover design by Maureen Moore
Ginger Cat's Booksmyth Press
www.thebooksmythpress.com

for you
from me

From form to content and back to form,
From norm to crazy and back to norm,

From bound to free and back to bound,
From sound to sense and back to sound.

So back and forth. It almost scares
A person the way things come in pairs.

Robert Frost "To a Thinker"

card tricks

how do you know?
        experience

how do you know?
        i'm not sure

now
        now

now?
        when?

now?
        not yet

        when?
now?

pick a card
    any card

here goes
    watch closely now

if you enjoy your thinking
      do you think your pleasure?

      gold sky
   lavender mist on the river

cousins meet and feast
     fond, funny memories

     thick wet air
       towel me off

     sleep meds work
damn, i'm hooked

     whistles in the wind
       truth rushes past

pink laurel
        pondside jewels

glossy green lake
smooth paddling

wine's gone
        pour the rum

movie menace
        mental solace

sad poems
            happy poet

tra la la la la la
        la la la la la la la

top dog
       alley cat

work late
no sleep

     love bug
   stinging hug

       now she's gone
     won't be back

placing stones
     jahrzeit

yellow orchid
       blooming still

change the oil
        vacuum the car

daughter home
talk till dawn

shuffle the deck
        burn the top card

skid marks in the grass
        racing lawn mowers

home late
        cold leftovers

card tricks are only card tricks
        and yet ...

polishing the tschatske
one by one

last spring love appeared
or was it two springs ago?

mama baba dada baba
baba baba baba baba baba baba

don't stop
high energy

don't stop
loving me

one more kiss
before you go

new friend? maybe ...
      maybe not

did you clean up after?
      midnight snack

      some believe
            some don't

      summer hug
            sweaty, sticky

            ask me first
please

big decision?
      flip a coin

fly high
       magnify

       can we help
each other?

       how do i help
              myself?

do you need
       my help?

       heat wave
         on goes the a. c.

expert misunderstands
       student misconstrues

"consider the tree"
                    philosophy lesson

        the tree
                        the forest

        the forest
                        the roots

        the tree
                        the house

        the tree
                        the coffin

        the tree
                        the god

read till 2 a.m.
                sleep

read till 2 a.m.
                woke up, light on

      raining
at last

      streams murmur
                northern appalachia

open-toed sandals
      crimson toenails

      slow walking
                hands in her pockets

how do you know?

           experience

how do you know?

i'm not sure

    now

        now

   now?

      when?

     now?

       not yet

         when?

      now?

now?
        patience

now?
        soon

rapt audience
        how will it end?

hop along
        sing a song

        practice, practice more
practice more

        music for her
                movie for him

inuktikut: "making love"
us: "laughing in bed"

lie down
　　　snuggle

　　　lie down
　　　　　giggle

midnight songs
　　　dawn prayers

piles of books
nothing to read

so sorry
　　　hakuna matata

little girl's a princess
mom's a queen

middle child
            never lonely

ten years old
innocent, open, happy

                summer heat
                        grilled meat

        physics fact
                the world's ice cream

easy street
        queasy street

                fourteen, home alone
                        not for long

lifetime learning
        approaching infinity

                for last 40 years
        almost no meat on my plate

reading in bed
        side by side

night ride
        keeping her company

sleeping late
saturday

she can't
        help herself

rust freckles
        stainless steel?

nerves tense?
        whiskey, please

                    the cut, the pain
                                    the blood

                    thursday lightning
        wind, rain

        driving home cross country
                    her van broke down in Omaha

                        she talks to things
            some talk back

                                lying down
        phone rings

                    da da da da!
            da da da da! da da da da

she ate
                    i talked

hiking with sticks in hands
                    4-legged march

                    after rain
happy plants

            circumambulating the yard
                    96 steps

                    late spring
                            peeper chorus

night trail
            walker's pal: flashlight

lower case
        democratic words

happy noisy kids
        breakfast to bedtime

stop, now!
        now, stop!

mid-summer eve
        late light

another day
        taller grass

he hates guns
        guns don't care

dry september
     easy harvest

new shirts
     cool shoes

forester 90 feet up
     tree wobbles, "help!"

friday night
　　　　bones tired

full summer moon
　　　lazing on the lawn

August evening
　　　　cricket tympani

stopping at the light
　　　waiting for the change

　　　　　soft lights
cozy home

herky jerky
　　　party dancing

nude painting
          love's memory

                    it's late
                              bedtime

appetite
          beyond hunger

frozen in a rut
          when will it thaw?

                              up early, o no
              out of coffee

              touching the goddess
sacred breasts

noo mu mamá
 boo hoo mamáma

  power
 who don't want some?

  humility
 path to power?

  cool night
crickets' veil of song thinning

 on earth
  angels exist

in heaven?
 who knows?

general dunks
          donut army

                    withdraw the troops
          bring in the bankers

owl hoots
               end of summer

          onion-soaked cashews
               tasty

do you dare
               do what you want?

          i've got the gold now
                    i wanna rule!

elders on bikes
strong knees

works all night
            sleeps all day

        going hunting?
                nah, swimming

        it's really truly about me
& me & me & me & me, too

        shake that pot
            popcorn pops

going out?
        bring your flask

i believe in not crossing
double yellow lines

douse the houseplants
        water the floor boards

            her knees ache
        desk work all day

giving birth, she screamed
        for all women and children

            chew gummies
        fall asleep

        place crash kills hundreds
            who's to blame?

27

            plane crash kills thousands
pilot's plan

            ask, listen
                    listen, ask

ask again
                    listen ...

                    sold their house
            got full price

            dig a hole
plant a flame bush

                    his body of work
dressed in praise

laid up
        for a while

                laid over
another day

        laid out
                for the viewing

                clean up
        after dinner

clean hands
                touch me close

        clean out
                the closet

ancient greed
      future grief

           no!
      i mean no!

no!
      no way!

          no!
don't ask again.

for the last time
          no!

how many times
      do i have to tell you no?

stop? go?
            no, baby, no

no. don't
stop now

        come and go
                eternal tango

        i'm "asbergerliano"
                    he sang

the king arrived
                nobody noticed

        do you know him?
i wish i did

outdoor concert
where's the audience?

sweeping up ribbons, crumbs
kids' party

can't stand, can't sit
aching back

she smoked, he didn't
she lived, he didn't

can't do this alone
or with others

my father?
dead many years

my mother?
i hear her prayers

your father?
your mother?

snowfall all over town
silent dusk

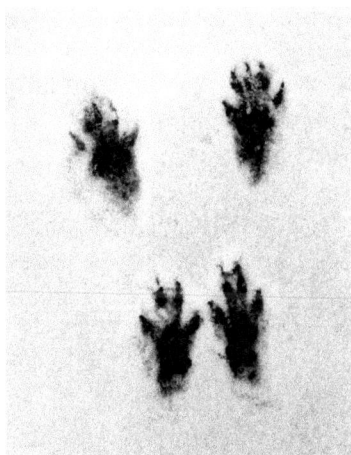

33

she laughs
    he laughs

    she laughs
       and laughs

he laughs
    and laughs

       they laugh
   and laugh

        you laugh
     i laugh

   we laugh
      and laugh

standing on the bridge
    icy water flows underfoot

    can't sleep
        counting toes

    staying home
feeling better

        pick me up
    i'll hold you

elephant in the room?
    a tiny statue

    her eyes
        hazel

she writes with a lilt
        gifted poet

up late
        sleeping in

        slept till 10
took a pill, slept some more

        ok now, go slow
shake it off

        heebie jeebes
slimy creepies

see this?
        a brand new deck

weeping boy
    his dog dead

        somebody dies
    stories linger

    autumn wind in the trees
cicadas fall silent

    woods road past the estate
      empty lane

    walk to town?
      a long way downhill

    planks delivered
      carpenters next

euphoric father
with his daughters

loving daughter
    takes him to dinner

sunrise
        deep green pines

talking with both sides
will they listen?

telling stories
revealing feelings

trying
failing

try, trying
keeps trying

make something
anything

waiting for the call
test results

book speaks patois
would you translate, please?

my favorite app
names trees and plants

i saw our faces
projected on a wall

doctor called
surgery tomorrow

sunday morning
pray or hike?

life's a serious business
so they claim

switching on the heat?
it's only september

it's just a game
    we love to play

is it this card?
    how about this one?

electric car?
solar panels?

halfway there
    going where?

one bright light
    biking at night

more and more
coming every day

more and more
        lost and gone

still adjusting
to being "me"

almost adjusted
        to loving you

            late night tv
good night's asleep

just woke up
what's new?

halfway there
          going where?

once i worked long and hard
      now i work, sometimes

     it ain't work, she says
i'm having fun

thin clouds
     bright moon

     lazy days
       10,000 ways

      wait
something new will happen

meatless meat
       mercy! plants alive!

       rainbows on the river
city lights

       a rainbow gleams
           in the dog's eye

at church
        napping on the pew

        wild woman
                soulful songs

        ducks huddle
frosty wind

        lost it all
                no matter now

        longest war
long forgotten

piles of books
        dust everywhere

abandoned fields
        mouse haven

bankrupt country club
            tall brown grass

october trees
            translucent woods

reading, writing
            stories never end

        no worries i say
uh oh, where'd my keys go?

blown away
            no need to rake

        stayed out all night
years ago

        do you believe?
           what?

           do you believe?
        sure

do you believe?
            do you?

        rainy sunday
           long-married sex

            time space
        nothing everything

guitars twang
old timey music

$20 bill on the street
gift from the muse

high leap
quick flop

software plods
hardware soards

remember the rabbit?
remember the turtle?

short prolific life
long scant life

crowded day
        solitary night

        look here
                nothing up my sleeve

        the womb
the grave

                pounding beat
        ecstatic dance

                washing
drying

        time t' let 'im go
                c'mon, let 'er rip

flash of imagination
at the speed of light

daydreaming
clear sky

up early
long trip ahead

free woman
      free man

      happy yesterday
happy tomorrow

boy's beauty
      woman's power

anxious
    calm

        awake
    asleep

   "spare a buck?"
"dig it, man"

do
            don't

        dig
deep

                    big
                dig

        hot diggity
diggety dog

                hot digetty
        dog diggety boom what you do

my wife
        best surprise of my life

goddess
divine child

old gods forgotten
old gods rise again

old gods risen
still have powers

kids' chatter
        happy family

    tie game
        teams played hard

what was that again?
          i forget

        found at last
    i want to stay lost

plant your feet
        you won't fall

silver sparks shower
        flesh-colored embers glow

she felt she'd been ill
　　all her long life

he's not afraid
he's terrified

take this spade
　　plant something

warm, sweet, devilish
　　　　i miss her

if only
　　she'd come back

　　were they really victims?
yes

gazing into each other's eyes
sighs

they loved
there were beloved

he tumbled
got up

all day long
one decision after another

who's in control?
of what?

grilled ribs smoke
some vegans choke

forgetting how
        to play the flirting game

go on, now
            no, not yet

        his lips ooze
                he can't stop lying

queen and jack of hearts
                my favorites

        she warned me
i didn't believe her

standing still
        clinging to the railing

pretty waitress grazed his hand
he tipped 50%

thinking nonsense
as usual

old neighbors moved out
new neighbors moved in

forest colors dazzle
autumn leaves splash the air

inside her pain, peace
if only i could share

one acorn
among billions

always on camera
everyday actor

she wore red
how did you miss her?

slow motion
strolling the woods path

she can't wait to hear
his story has her in thrall

why do we do
only what we do well?

when she can, she does
what lures her

if you give me three
      i'll hold two for you

      it's a club and it's a ten
what? it's not?

      look close
tiny critters, tiny blossoms

      can't see what's coming?
my eyes stunned by light

poet pities his life
      turn the page

      poet rages
savor the pages

poet sings sad songs
              ragged voice

        2 a.m. can't sleep
ambien, please

              long night
        short sleep

"phlogiston"
not in today's dictionary

not too tall
        not too small

inhale
        free

exhale
        risen

lost sock
        won't ever be found

vague outlines
        distant hums

bake chocolate cake
  lick spoon, lick bowl

  optimism
    cures many ills

    life is good
      most days

run, run
    quell the pain

          goodbye
my dear old bookshop

    need help?
      i'm available

almost home
        i wonder who's there

            outside dark
                icy rain

inside bright
            warm, dry

decades later
        old friends meet

old friends meet
        what to say, what to say

old friends meet
        what to do, what to do

losing weight?
        eating water

    right now
        more than ever

    one forgets
the other forgives

    fear a blight?
        build your cache

storage locker
        so much stuff

    toxic waste forever or
        carbon emissions?

it's all over now
what's next?

pale sun
        november light

he jumped
        as did his dad

truck trailer
        cheap retirement

venture forth at last
        gone shopping

discount food
        shelf-life long past

pale sun
    December light

   so what?
            right?

nostalgia
    retirement classic

picnic by the waterfall
        caring for the old ones

riding home at midnight
        "Mad Dog" at the wheel

    whew
        it's almost over now

10 degrees outside
        stiff knees

    80 degrees
happy bees

    rah rah shish boom bah
rah rah lah di da dah ... lah di dah

young man
100 wrong decisions

older man
1000 wrong decisions

old man
enough decisions

you were far away
i came for you

what i see in your eyes
is what i want

can't sleep together
can't sleep apart

        recovered from surgery
she loved me then

winter lake
                crackling ice

        broke up
she took our oak table & chairs

        longing for her
                lingers in his toes

        do good
                good's ample

every human is holy
        is every demon holy?

rattler on the trail
        hikers rush to see

        fresh bread
    little girl ate the whole loaf

if you'd done this
        you'd have done it better

          bounding down the stairs
we bumped hips

dark curtains closed
          street sounds soften

          he biked across the park
               she was waiting

something said
          something else said

          separate 40 years
               they still weep together

death sails the world
               in a virus fleet

harsh winds
		branches crash

			systole
					diastole

boomlay boomlay boomlay boom
	boomlay boomlay boomlay BOOM

				what does he see?
		he's free

he's all fired up
		watch out now!

			it's not just day or night
				or love or hate

she grasps it
    she can't hold on

    impossible?
        possible

    I thought
he was original

why do they hate her?
    she's korean, too beautiful

    it's a diamond
      and it's an ace

I could use a nap
    lazy, as always

intense days, these
       to say the least

      you did what?
            i've done lots worse

wash your hands
        keep them still

      exposed?
          everyone's exposed

topical?
       internal?

      you, go
        see, me

night rain
morning fields shine

kids learn and leave
abandoned farms

ethanol
corn farmers' friend

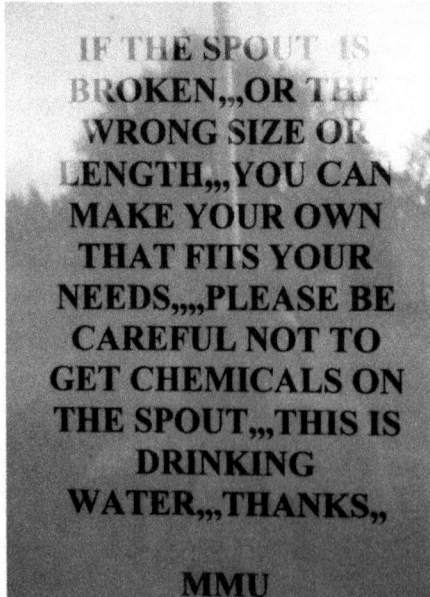

IF THE SPOUT IS
BROKEN,,,OR THE
WRONG SIZE OR
LENGTH,,,YOU CAN
MAKE YOUR OWN
THAT FITS YOUR
NEEDS,,,,PLEASE BE
CAREFUL NOT TO
GET CHEMICALS ON
THE SPOUT,,,THIS IS
DRINKING
WATER,,,THANKS,,

MMU

calling your friends
    telling your love

melting snow
    dripping eaves

        the spring woods
            peeper symphony

        lie down
            rest up

wait in line
                fly home

        lay low
            dream high

everybody knows it's not real
   nobody really knows

   bored? alone?
        gotta get out?

        in the quiet store
hard eyes above masks

   let's take a walk
opposite sides of the path

        wait – i love you
   I know, see you later

"oo ee oo ah ah
        ting tang walla walla bing bang"

it's new
i want it

it's old
i'll keep it

dancing alone
holding it together

balancing a ladder on his chin
how?

driving west from a man's death
following sundogs home

danger appeals
it don't compel

the future is now
        you kidding?

let's wait
        till morning

        let's wait
                it out

we waited
        and we waited

        I can wait
                as long as you need

        don't wait
last chance for the last dance

boozey loosey
     doozey snoozey

we know now
     what prayer is for

     I think I feel
          pretty good, maybe

night cruising
     long curves

you like going fast?
          better slow down

     wally wahoo
          wally wally wahoo

uh oh – old habit
        we shook hands

      if you want to talk
        call me

i see
        i can't believe

i believe
        i don't need to see

      i listen
        i don't understand

      i'm getting up there ...
        what more can i do?

soul mates?
          missed each other

               soul mates
                         always

once he was hot
          she still is

          soul mate?
               passed on by

                    soul mates
          the lucky have many

up late
          foolin around

you're magic
              so are you

          so long
                  later, gator

          bye for now
ciao

          bon nuit
                  bis morgens

hasta mañana
          sleep well

          good night
                  sweet dreams

now you see it

now you don't

Photo Credits

Page 15: Princess photo taken at 3 Sisters Sanctuary, Goshen, MA.

Page 21: Photo is of Ben Niles who climbed and cut down 80', 90', and 100' Eastern Hemlocks leaning over our house.

Page 50: Photo by Danny Timmins, profile of Ocean Timmins.

Text Credits

Page 73: Ross Bagdasarian, "Witch Doctor" (1958).

Page 78: Vachel Lindsay, "The Congo" (1914). This was the first poem I performed in public in 1961.

For other moving and surprising books of
poems, fiction, and graphic tales, please visit
www.thomastimmins.com

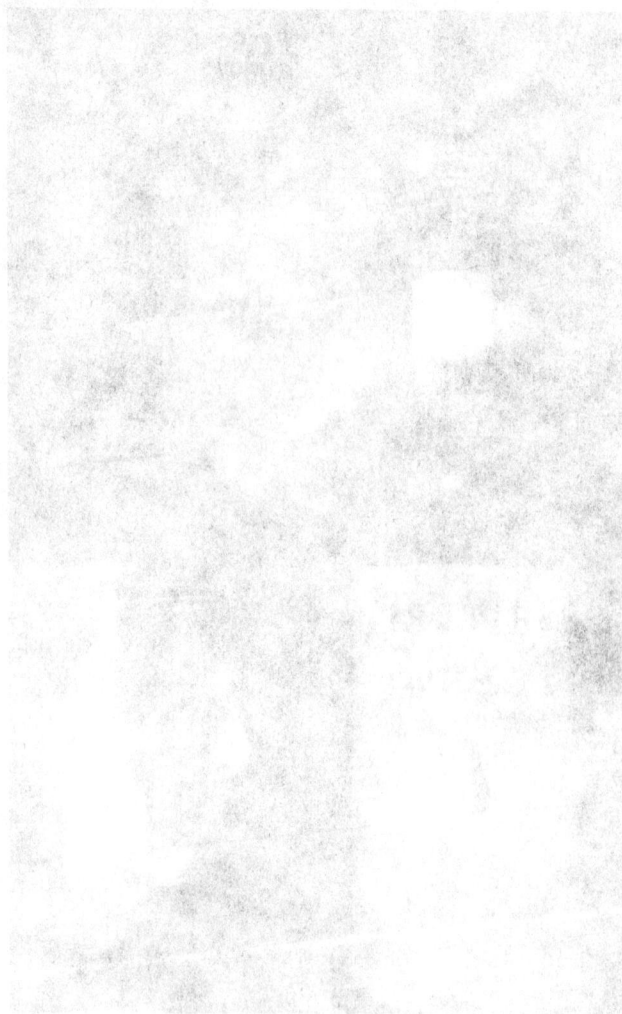

couplets here, couplets there
couplets everywhere